Feng Shui Beginner

How To Create Good Energy Flow With Basics Of Feng Shui In Your Home

Table of Contents

Introduction

I would like to thank you for making a choice to read my book, *"Feng Shui for Beginner: How to create good energy flow with Basics of Feng Shui in your home"*.

This book will give you comprehensive information on how to create good energy flow with the basics of Feng Shui in your home.

Have you ever stopped to think that the way things around your home are arranged could have a profound effect on your happiness, prosperity, luck and a lot more? Well, if you didn't, now you know. And why is that? Well, this has everything to do with being a reflection of the energy, which the environment around us produces.

All that is the core of a 6000+ year old Chinese practice, which is now taking root in the western world thanks to its amazing benefits when it comes to influencing the environment around you to attract success, prosperity, positive energy and luck.

What if you could learn how to do that? What if I could teach you how to get the environment around you to work for you as you strive to attract the things you've always wanted?

Well, this book would help you learn basic knowledge of Feng Shui. At the end of the book, you'll be able to understand, arrange and organize your home to create good energy.

Thanks again for downloading this book, I hope you enjoy it!

A Basic Understanding

What Is It?

Feng Shui is an intricate traditional Chinese art that is based on an attempt to fully grasp and understand the dynamic flow of energy through the universe. It studies the way people are influenced and affected by the environment in which they dwell and also recognizes the connection between a person's inner being and his external surroundings.

The whole motive behind embracing Feng Shui is to try to introduce some specific, positive changes and adjustments to your surroundings so as to make your environment work for you and not against you. These changes are usually made around the living and working environment.

Traditional Chinese practitioners held the belief that the degree of success or failure, which a person is likely to achieve in life, is dependent on a number of factors, some within control and some beyond control.

These five factors include:

- Luck

- Knowledge

- Destiny/Fate

- Personal factors and choices

- Feng Shui

In English, Feng Shui means 'wind' and 'water', which stands for harmony and balance. These two elements (wind and water) are highly regarded since they are believed to have immense energy, which can influence human life and various other mortals. In China, they are often associated with luck. While Feng Shui has a Chinese origin, it is increasingly gaining popularity around the world thanks to its scientific as well as its artistic integration.

Feng Shui is a 6000-year old art that is based on the belief that energy, which is also referred to as 'chi', flows through the universe and has an impact on our day-to-day lives.

This ancient Chinese art and science seeks to make you more compatible and in harmony with nature, your surroundings and your daily life so as to positively affect all areas of your life including your emotions, finances and health. Ancient Chinese culture believed that smooth waters and gentle wind result in an abundant harvest and good health whereas stagnant water and coarse winds are believed to bring diseases, famine and chaos. This is where good and bad feng shui come in. Good Feng Shui in this case brings good fortune and prosperity whereas bad feng shui brings about hardships, struggles, and bad luck. While you may think of this as some superstitious idea, the truth is that going with nature rather than against it will bring good fortune to you and the environment. For instance, if you surround yourself in a room that vibrates negative energy (from the negative things that happen in there for instance), this room will always be the fertile ground for nurturing suffering whether financial, health, relationship etc. The concept is that if you enclose yourself with negative symbols or get positive symbols placed in the wrong way, this may probably attract misfortune. This simply means that where every item in the house is placed and the way it is placed makes a difference on whether it will attract or vibrate good chi that will in turn bring good feng shui. The placement of furniture, buildings, rooms and even yourself can have a profound effect on whether you will attract good feng shui or not.

Feng shui is cognizant of the fact that our emotional and physical environment affect our lives greatly such that if you surround yourself with symbols of negation, contempt and indifference towards nature and life, and end up choosing to live in areas that are pretty much repugnant to our human soul, we end up attracting misfortune. For instance, hard edges, uncomfortable furniture, and clutter create what is referred to as shar or just sha, which ideally means bad energy in Chinese. But if you were to replace concrete, noise, and mess or any other unpleasant elements for cleanliness, organization and objects that express the sweet things in life like art, beauty and order, you attract good feng shi. If any area has broken objects, mess and negative images, these are likely to weaken or block chi (life force). So if you live in an area with such features, you are likely to have a weakened chi i.e. sha or shar chi. In essence, shar chi is brought about by anything that creates shadows, has sharp or intrusive edges, dirties the water or air or is stagnant. On the other hand, stuff that create good chi include bright lights, plants, moving objects such as electric fans, mobiles, wind chimes, microwaves etc.

Feng Shui lays out some basic guidelines for how a home should be built, arranged, and decorated in order to attract positive energy, good luck, and prosperity

Although chi is literally everywhere, there are places that have higher concentrations of chi (whether good or bad). This has a lot to do with the landscape characteristics. For instance, fast moving water is believed to bring bad fortune. Additionally, living in areas that have excessive exposure to strong winds is recipe for bad fortune. The logic behind this is that this swift moving water or wind carries the good chi away.

Feng Shui has been a traditional way of life for Asians for several centuries. It has deeply influenced the way Asian houses, cities, villages and even cemeteries are built. For instance, Asians avoid building their homes in such a way that their gate faces a T-junction because it is believed to attract negative energy and bad luck.

The opposite is true. Slow moving water (maybe a meandering river) is believed to attract good chi. The same applies to rolling hills; they create and collect good chi. This is believed to bring happiness, prosperity and longevity to the residents.

Basic Feng Shui Concepts

To fully understand Feng Shui, there are a few basic concepts surrounding the art, which you must understand such as the Yin and Yang theory, the concept of Chi, feng shui colors and the five natural elements.

The Yin and Yang Theory

Feng Shui operates based on the fundamental principles of Yin and Yang. Yin and Yang represent balance and continual change and is the foundation on which the whole theory of Feng Shui is built.

Yin and Yang are two opposite energies that are dependent on each other and must always be in balance. They are mutually dependent opposites and cannot survive without each other.

The theory of Yin and Yang was developed by the Taoists thousands of years ago. It was used to explain the constantly changing nature of the universe. Nature is believed to be an endless cycle of polar opposites. For instance, day and night, work and rest, heat and cold, moisture and dryness: everything in nature exhibits varying combinations of good and bad.

Yin, which means "Shady Side", exhibits the nurturing qualities of darkness, cold, moisture, rest, and structure while Yang displays energetic qualities such as light, heat, function, activity, and dryness. It refers to the "Sunny Side".

Therefore, to have good Feng Shui in any environment, a balance of Yin and Yang must always be maintained. There mustn't be too much of one or the other such that the natural equilibrium is upset.

The Concept of Chi

Chi, is the word used to describe the universal energy that emerges from everything around us. In Feng Shui, it refers to energy that flows in the body and energy that flows around the environment. It is a combination of real and metaphysical forces such as energy that flows from the earth's magnetic field, the quality of air that surrounds us, sunlight, color vibrations, cosmic influences, the nature of thoughts and emotions and the form of objects.

Traditional Chinese practitioners believe that Chi influences the way a place feels and the way the people in that surrounding would feel.

The goal of Feng Shui is to control the Chi in an environment especially in your home and office such that good and fresh Chi is able to flow within your environment and within your body.

Feng Shui seeks to promote the flow of Sheng Chi, which is good quality Chi energy and avoid the flow of Sha and Si Chi, which refers to bad quality energy or, Chi, which is believed to cause depression and bring bad luck.

The Five Natural Elements

The five natural elements are the symbolic basis on which the whole concept of Feng Shui is built. They are also known as the five phases and each of the five elements relates to a specific compass direction, metaphoric representation, season, color, shape, body part, aspiration or family member.

They are used in different ways to influence, control, manage, enhance, support, or weaken one another. The five elements in Feng Shui are wood, earth, fire, metal, and water.

Feng Shui seeks to balance the environment by getting as many of the five elements to work together.

Feng Shui Colors

Colors are a very important concept in Feng Shui. Color represents vibration; every color has its own unique frequency and the same way you are connected to the energy in your home, you are also connected to the colors around your home.

Color has a great impact on your physical and psychological well-being and you can use colors to affect your life positively. For instance, if you want to attract love, you should use colors that represent and attract romance.

1. **Red**: Red in Feng Shui represents the fire element. It is used to attract relationships/romance, prosperity and fame, and is best used in the bedroom, living room, dining room or kitchen.

2. **Orange:** Orange also represents the fire element although it is less intense and much more cheerful than red. It is great for use in interior spaces where you don't want

to use red. It also attracts relationships, reputation and prosperity like red, and can be used in the living room, kitchen, dining room, and bedroom.

3. **Yellow**: Yellow is another color that represents the fire element and can be used to attract the same things, and in the same areas as red or orange.

4. **Green**: Green naturally has a calming and relaxing psychological effect and in Feng Shui, it represents the wood element. It is best used in the bathroom and can attract good health, knowledge, or skills.

5. **Blue**: Blue represents the water element. It is also best used in the bathroom to attract abundance and prosperity, knowledge and career growth.

6. **Purple**: Purple is best used in the bedroom and is believed to attract abundance and prosperity.

7. **Black:** Black also represents the water element. It is best used as an accessory color to attract helpful people, knowledge, career growth, and success in journeys and travels.

8. **White**: White represents the metal element. It represents purity and cleanliness and is best used in the bathroom to attract helpful people and promote creativity especially in children.

9. **Grey**: Grey also represents the metal element and is best used as an accessory color to attract helpful people, success in travels, creativity, and knowledge.

10. **Brown:** Brown represents the earth element and can be used in the bedroom or living room to attract skills/knowledge.

11. **Pink**: Pink is used in the bedroom to attract love and romance.

Why Feng Shui Works

Feng Shui is not just some fairy concept; it is a very effective tool that works and here is why:

1. **It Improves Positive Energy in Your Home**: Everything in life contains energy; even that chair you're sitting on. Some energy is positive and uplifting while some are negative and stagnating.

   Since everything contains energy, your home (or office) is a vibrating field of energy and since you are also made of energy, you are connected to your home and you and your home are connected to a larger unified energy field in the universe.

The more positive energy in your surroundings, the more positive things you'll attract into your life and vice versa.

2. **Feng Shui Enhances the Power of Intention**: If you've read Rhonda Byrne's "*The Secret*", you would understand how important the power of intention and imagination is. Your intention determines what you attract. Just by making some changes and additions to your home, you can program positive affirmations in your environment and within your subconscious that helps you attract the things you want.

3. **Feng Shui Helps Nourish Your Spirit, Mind and Body**: One of the places where you can truly get to be yourself, is your home. Your home is where you get to renew your mind and emotions after a hard day's job; it is where you get to dream and discover your full potential. It is a meeting place for the physical, the emotional, and the spiritual.

When you apply Feng Shui in your home, it helps you convert your home into a sacred place where you can truly discover your potentials and nurture your body, spirit and soul.

Just Before You Feng Shui Your Home

In the next few chapters, you are going to learn how to apply the principles of Feng Shui to all areas in your home to attract good chi in your life and home.

There are a few things you need to know before that:

1. **Understand The Power You Possess**: The world we live in is not solid and inanimate like most people believe. It is actually slippery, variable, and molded by your thoughts, personal energy, feelings, and beliefs.

   You have to understand that you are much more powerful than you think you are, and you are an architect of your fortunes or misfortunes. You have to understand that you are connected to your environment through your energy and you can shape your future when you know how to control the flow of Chi within and around you.

2. **Have a Clear Intention**: You have to make your intentions and purpose clear. Why have you decided to embrace Feng Shui? What do you want to attract- money? Love? Power? It is only when you have a clear intention that you can make the correct adjustments with Feng Shui, in order to attract what you want.

3. **Declutter**: You cannot truly do Feng Shui without first clearing clutter from your home. If you're not ready to let go of the unnecessary stuff, then don't bother with Feng Shui. When you clear out clutter, it promotes free flow of positive chi around you. When there is too much of clutter, flow of chi is limited.

4. **Keep Your Home Clean and Organized**: It's not just clutter that attracts negative chi in the home; dirt and dust are also major culprits. To attract good Chi, you have to keep your surrounding clean and organized at all times.

5. **Take Things Slowly**: Take your time. Don't make drastic changes that would leave you frustrated at the end of the day. Applying Feng Shui to your home must be

done slowly, consistently and with strong and clear intentions.

A Timeline Showing How Feng Shui Has Evolved

1. Chou Dynasty (1122-207 BC): The Emperor Wen used pa kua (also known as bagua) to discover and define patterns of change.

2. 8th century BC: The Chinese used pa kua as a compass coupled with the theory of change to design, built and structure cities, kingdoms, ancient buildings etc. This was also used to bring peace, prosperity, and wealth to the nation.

3. 206 BCE-219 CE, during the Han dynasty: *Kan Yu* was used to study the energy of various landforms and how they affect those who live or stay around them.

4. Chin Dynasty (265-420 CE): The ordinary folk in China started using Feng Shi. Originally, it was a preserve of the emperors, the royal families, the rich, and the mighty. They used what was referred to as kan yu when selecting estates for themselves.

5. Tang and Sung dynasties, 618-906 CE and 960-1279CE: The period of golden Kan yu.

This period saw the use of geomantic compass, which was referred to as lo-p'an.

6. Emperor Hsü Jen-wang of the Sung dynasty then expanded the then practice of Feng Shui in that he started applying it to diagnose buildings and landforms. He ended up forming what's referred to flying stars system of Feng Shui or Mysterious Subtleties or simply Hsüan-k'ung.

7. Ch'ing dynasty (1644-1911) and the period of the Republic of China (1911-1949). This period saw the introduction of the Pa-chai (Eight Mansions) School by Jo-kuan Tao-jen. Then another school referred to as San-yüan. Currently, there are 4 main schools of Chinese Feng Shui namely Pachai, San-ho, San-yüan and Hsüan-k'ung. Any of the newer feng shui schools, including western feng shui is a product of these 4.

Now that you have some good background information on what feng shui is all about, its principles, why it works and how it came into being, let's now implement feng shui in different parts of your house. In the subsequent chapters, we will discuss how to unleash the full power of feng shui in different parts of your home.

Entrance (Face Of The Home)

One of the most important areas in your home to Feng Shui, is your front door. Your front door is the entrance to your home and it represents the mouth of Chi; the point through which all Chi energy flows into your home.

Your front door is very vital to your happiness and well being hence it is extremely important to ensure that your front door not only looks good but also feels good and supports your personal intentions.

Colors for Your Front Door

According to the Classical Feng Shui, the most appropriate color to use for the entrance of your home would depend on the direction of the door and its corresponding earth element.

1. **East Facing Door**: The East area is synonymous with the wood element hence if your front door is facing the east, the most appropriate colors to use would be colors that are synonymous with the wood element such as green or brown.

   In Feng Shui, water element and earth elements nourishes wood elements (think of how plants need water and soil to survive), so you can also complement with water element colors such as blue and black or earth element colors such as light yellow.

2. **Southeast Facing Doors**: If your front door is facing the Southeast, the best colors to use are colors that represent the wood element because in Feng Shui, the Southeast is also synonymous with the wood element. Green and brown are the most suitable colors but you can also complement with water element colors such as black and blue or earth elements like yellow and sandy colors.

3. **South Facing Doors**: South facing doors are best painted with colors that represent the fire element such as strong pink, orange, yellow or purple. You can also complement with wood element colors (wood fuels fire) such as green and brown.

4. **South**: South facing doors are best painted with colors that represent the fire element such as strong pink, orange, yellow, or purple. You can also complement with wood element colors (wood fuels fire) such as green and brown.

5. **Southwest:** If your door is facing the southwest, you should choose colors that represent the earth element such as light

yellow, earthy, or sandy colors. You can also complement with colors that represent the fire element such as strong yellow, rich pink, red, purple, or deep orange.

6. **West:** The most suitable colors to use when your front door is facing the west are colors that represent the metal element such as white and grey. Complementary colors include colors that represent the earth elements such as light yellow and sandy colors.

7. **Northwest**: Doors facing the northwest are best painted with colors that represent the metal element such as white and grey and complemented with earth element colors like light yellow and sandy colors.

8. **North**: For your north facing doors, use colors that represent the water element like black and blue and complement with metal element colors like white and grey.

9. **Northeast:** The Northeast direction is synonymous with the earth element so you should consider using corresponding colors and complement with fire element colors like red, deep orange, purple, or strong yellow.

Decorating Your Front Door (Main Entry Point)

Like I mentioned earlier, your front door/main entrance point is the mouth of Chi and if you want to create good Feng Shui in your home, you must first start with your front door/main entry.

We already talked about choosing the appropriate colors for your front door. Now we're going to focus on how to decorate your front door to promote good Feng Shui.

Just like colors, the type of decoration to use for your front door depends on the direction it is facing.

1. **East/Southeast**: First, you should choose colors that are synonymous with the wood element then complement with decorations that represent or nourish the wood element.

   Use health, vibrant green plants placed in flowerpots that are green, blue, black, or earthy in color. It's also great to use a water fountain around your main entry point to represent the water element. Use rocks to represent the earth energy and a jute mat with rectangular shape to represent the wood element.

Always avoid using decorations or items that represent the metal elements, such as metal pots or round shaped decoration as well as items that represent the fire element such as red colored doormats, red colored flowerpots or triangular shaped décor materials.

2. **South**: If your main entry is facing the south, you should use colors that represent the fire element and then support with decorations that nourish the fire element. Use green, healthy vibrant plants in red, brown, green, or purple colored pots. Use a jute doormat in rectangle or triangular shape.

   For your south facing entryway, you should avoid items that represent the earth or water element such as clay pots, black or blue colored flowerpots, décor with wavy shapes, or square shaped décor.

3. **Southwest/Northeast**: Doors or entryways facing the southwest or the northeast are best painted with colors that represent the Feng Shui earth elements such as orange, red, purple, pink and yellow. You should also use decorations that represent the earth element such as

earthenware pots and triangular shaped doormats.

Avoid any décor materials that represent the metal elements such as metal pots and round shaped décor, those that represent the wood elements such as big plants and green décor and those that represent the water element.

4. **West/Northwest**: If your entryway is facing the west or the northwest, use a color that represents the metal element and then decors that represent the earth element as well such as metal pots, square shaped doormats, or metal hardware on the door.

You should avoid the fire or water elements as much as possible.

5. **North**: North-facing doorways work well with the Feng Shui water element. Use colors such as white, blue, black and gray while avoiding colors like brown, green, red or purple.

Use decorative materials that support the water elements such as water fountains, metal hardware, and blue or black colored doormats or metal containers and pots.

Avoid using decorative materials that represent the fire element such as red doormats, triangular shaped items, and red colored flowerpots and avoid items that represent the earth element like clay pots, square shaped items and rocks.

It is important to ensure that your entryway is very beautiful and inviting. It should also be kept free of clutter and properly lit at all times.

Living Room

There's nothing complicated about creating good Feng Shui in your living room. The rules are simple; your living room has to be comfortable, relaxing, and welcoming.

Your living room is a reflection of your true personality and has an effect on the relationship and connection you would have with people within and outside your home.

Choosing Appropriate Feng Shui Colors for Your Living Room

You have to choose colors for the living room while putting every member of the family into consideration because the living room is where every member of the home comes together to connect and relax. The colors you choose must be enjoyable by every member of the family.

A color like brown would promote peace and stability within the home while a color like yellow would foster better communication and openness.

Good Feng Shui colors to use for your living room include gold, chocolate, cream, brown, honey, bronze, earth orange, tan, earthy yellow, earthy red, coral, peach, and terra cotta.

Furniture Placement

Furniture placement in the living room is another very important aspect of Feng Shui. Furniture must be placed in a way that fosters better communication and promotes flow of good Chi.

Adopt a circular method of arranging your furniture such that none of your chairs have their backs to the door or if that is impossible, hang a mirror on the wall in such a way that anyone that has their back to the door can easily see people going out or coming in through the door.

Avoid placing your sofas directly in front of the door because it causes energy to flow directly at anyone seated there, causing them discomfort.

The largest piece of furniture (sofa) should be placed in a command position. The command position is the space facing the door and off to the side. This enhances flow of Chi.

Avoid bad furniture arrangements in the living room such as L-shaped arrangements, disjointed arrangements, and floating arrangements.

Decoration

Portraits: In your living room, you should hang a large portrait of family members as a way to stress the importance of each family member.

Chandeliers: Use a crystal chandelier to keep your living room well lit.

Animal Decorations: You may use pictures or carvings of animals in your living room but you should completely avoid the use of pictures or carvings of fierce or aggressive animals.

Space: Ensure that your living room is very spacious. Chi must have enough space to move around.

Shelves: Shelves placed in the living room must not be exposed. They should have covers or doors to avoid killing energy.

Doors: It's best to have just one door or not more than 2 doors in your living room. If you have more than one door, its best to keep the other doors closed.

Windows: Keep the ratio of windows to doors at 3:1. If you have too many windows, use your curtains to hide them.

Activating the Five Feng Shui Elements in Your Living Room

Southeast: This area should be enhanced with water elements. You can make use of aquariums or water features. You can make use of aquariums or water features, blue curtains, blue rugs or blue cushions. This helps to increase wealth.

South: This area is synonymous with the fire element and is believed to bring recognition and fame luck. Activate the fire element in this area by using red curtains, red lights, and red cushions.

Southwest: This area is also synonymous with the fire element. It is also believed to attract good relationships and romance. Enhance this area with crystal chandeliers and red colored décor.

East: Use wood element décor to bring health luck. You could use cane furniture, potted plants, or flowers in this area.

West: This area is synonymous with metal and represents family relationships. You can enhance harmonious family relationships by hanging portraits of your family members in this area.

Northeast: Activate the health element in the northeast area of your living room to improve education luck for your kids. You could make use of crystals or table lamps in this area.

North: The north area helps to attract good luck in your career. Activate this area with water elements like oil paintings of waterfalls.

Northwest: This area represents the luck of the breadwinner of the house. Use white and grey painted walls or curtains to activate this area. Completely avoid the use of red in this area.

Kitchen

In Feng Shui, the kitchen is a very important area of the home. Food symbolizes health and wealth and cooking also represents a daily representation of your good fortune, abundance, and the earth's infinite resources.

Your kitchen is also a strong activating force for abundance and prosperity because it is represented by the fire element.

The first rule for creating good Feng Shui in your kitchen is cleanliness. Everything in your kitchen should always be kept clean, no leftover food or dirty dishes lying around.

Your kitchen should also be airy. There should be a radiation of Chi around the kitchen and the meals you prepare.

Keep your kitchen clean and free of clutter.

Choosing Feng Shui Kitchen Colors

The most appropriate Feng Shui colors to use for your kitchen include red, orange, yellow, raspberry, burgundy, coral, earthy red, terra-cotta, maroon, honey, rust and salmon.

The most important thing is to choose colors that express health, vitality, and happiness.

Furniture and Appliances Placement

Correct furniture and appliance placement in the kitchen is also important for good Feng Shui.

Here are a few important tips for appliance placement in your Feng Shui kitchen.

- Avoid placing your stove (or gas cooker) beside your sink. Your stove should be as far away from your sink as possible. This is because the stove is synonymous with the fire element and your sink is synonymous with the water element. The water element neutralizes the fire element (think of how water is used to extinguish fire). Therefore, you can't place them beside each other. The same thing goes for every other thing that is synonymous with the water element in your kitchen such as your fridge.

- Place a mirror on the wall above your stove to create an illusion of additional space and stimulate the flow of chi through the kitchen space. If you don't want to use a mirror, you can make use of glossy wall tiles. This helps to attract wealth and prosperity in the home.

- Don't place your cabinets or kitchen décor items in sharp corners. This would attract negative energy and cause stagnation of Chi. You should also avoid using decorating accessories with sharp edges in your kitchen. Sharp objects and kitchen utensils like knives, should always be kept in drawers or closed boxes.

- Throw out all broken and useless items as they block the flow of Chi.

- Place your stove (or gas cooker) in a position such that anyone cooking would have their back facing the door. This is called the command position in Feng Shui and it helps to attract prosperity.

- Don't use any pictures of family or friends in your kitchen and avoid placing magnets on your fridge as they promote bad Chi.

Bath Room

In Feng Shui, the bathroom symbolizes purification and renewal. It is a place where you can get to release unwanted things from your life. Good Feng Shui bathrooms must be well-lit, properly ventilated, and kept fresh and clean at all times.

Choosing the Best Bathroom Colors

Green and blue are considered good Feng Shui bathroom colors. Blue is synonymous with the water element and represents cleansing and purification while green is synonymous with the earth element and represents new beginnings and growth. Another great color to use in your bathroom is white; white represents purity and cleanliness.

Feng Shui Bathroom Locations

There are a few very bad locations for your bathroom in Feng Shui. Some of them include:

1. **A Bathroom at the center of your home**: This is considered bad because the center of the home is regarded as the yin-yang point and must be free and open. If your bathroom is at the center of the house

and you are unable to relocate it, you should do the following:

- Always keep it clean and free of clutter.

- Beautify your bathroom with candles and flowers to promote good Feng Shui.

- Use air-purifying plants to improve the quality of air in your bathroom. You can also use an aromatherapy diffuser.

- Avoid having the same flat quality of light in your bathroom. You can use a dimmer switch to introduce alternating levels of light.

- Activate the earth or fire elements in your bathroom. This would help to absorb the excess water element in your bathroom.

2. **A Bathroom Facing Your Front Door**: A bathroom facing your front door is also considered bad Feng Shui. Your front door is the point where Chi flows into your home and a bathroom facing your front door helps good Chi to escape without fully circulating and nourishing the entire home. If your bathroom is facing your front door, you can still remedy the situation and

promote good Feng Shui by doing the following:

- Ensure that the bathroom door is always kept close to avoid escape of Chi.

- Take time to create strong and good Feng Shui in your front door. If your front door has good chi, the chances of losing good chi through your front door facing bathroom would be lower.

- Create a very strong Feng Shui focal point at your front door and in other areas of your home where you want Chi to flow to, in order to promote the flow through the home and prevent escape of Chi.

3. **A Bathroom Facing Your Kitchen**: A bathroom door facing your kitchen is considered bad Feng Shui too. The energy of the bathroom, which represents release and purification, should not interact with the energy of the kitchen, which represents nourishment and warmth.

For good Feng Shui, you must have your kitchen and bathroom as far away from each other as possible. However, if you are unable to change the location of your bathroom, you can apply the following remedies:

- Always keep your bathroom clean and comfortable.

- Define the boundary between your kitchen and bathroom with a bamboo curtain, a tall plant, or a door without glass.

- Use separate colors for painting the two opposing walls as a way to define the separate area.

4. **A Bathroom above Your Bedroom**: Some homes have architectural designs that allow the bathrooms to be located above the bedroom. This is also a bad Feng Shui set-up. You can remedy this by:

- Using a strong fire element in the bathroom.

- Having design features on the ceiling that helps to create a barrier between the energies in the bathroom and the bedroom. You can use ceiling light fixtures or crown moldings.

5. **A Bathroom over the Front Door**: Another bad Feng Shui bathroom location

is a bathroom that is located above the front door. You can remedy this bad Feng Shui situation by:

- Clearing out clutter

- Creating a solid separation between both spaces. Use deep color flooring or bathroom rug in your upper bathroom.

- Keep the bathroom door closed at all times.

- Use lighting fixtures like crystal chandeliers in your main entryway to strengthen the division between both spaces.

- Maintain good Feng Shui in your entryway.

Bedroom & Children's room

The bedroom is another important part of the house. Most people spend the most of their time in the bedroom relaxing and rejuvenating their minds and bodies; hence, the bedroom must be made into a personal sanctuary. It must be kept comfortable, serene, cozy, and restful.

Choosing Feng Shui Bedroom Colors

Choose colors that are warm and serene and accentuate with calm and romantic colors. Great colors for the bedroom include brown, beige, cream, earth tones, lavender, and pink.

Don't use colors like blue, green or white or colors that are too cool as they would reduce intimacy or sensuality in the room.

Your bed should have space on both sides. You should also keep underneath the bed free of clutter.

If you're looking to attract romance into your life, don't use solitary images, use images that promote equality and partnership. For instance, if you must use a bedside lamp; don't just use one lamp stand on either side of the bed; use two lamps on both sides.

Your bed should also be placed in a position of power. It must be as far away from the door as possible but must also allow you to be able to see the door clearly. If it's impossible to achieve this, place a mirror in a position that allows you see the reflection of the door from your bed.

Another thing to avoid is placing your bed in line with the door. It causes the Chi flowing from the door to flow directly to your bed, causing health problems and sleep disruptions.

If you must use images, use images that are calm and relaxing and helps you to feel safe. You can also use the under listed tips to create a good Feng Shui bathroom.

1. Ensure that your bed has a solid headboard.

2. Don't use photos of people watching you e.g. photos of friends, religious leaders or even family members.

3. Ensure that there are no heavy objects hanging over your head.

4. Position your mirror away from your bed so it doesn't reflect your sleeping form.

5. Don't place your bed under a window.

6. Take all electrical equipment, TV's or computer out of the bedroom or at least hide them when not in use.

7. Don't use live plants or flowers in your bedroom.

8. Avoid using water elements or images in your bedroom as well.

Children's Room

Your children's room should be painted and enhanced with colors that make them calm and peaceful such as warm pastels and rich colors.

Don't use primary colors to paint your children's room as it makes them hyperactive.

Hang awards, plaques, or artworks by your children in their room as a way to boost their self-esteem. Place family photos to boost sense of love and security.

Lastly, it is important to teach your children the importance of simple living and letting go of things that may create clutter in their living and working spaces.

Conclusion

Feng Shui works and since I discovered it, I now know my living elements are set to invite and create good energy. That special feeling, brings me complete happiness, prosperity and energetic motivation comes from within. I also think that those positive feeling from good Feng Shui is effecting my physical and mental health better than it has been before that I implemented Feng Shui.

Why not try it? I'm certain you wont regret it later.

Thank you for taking your precious time to read this book! I hope this book was able to help you to understand the basic concept of Feng Shui and how you can implement it in your home.

Finally, if you enjoyed this book, would you be kind enough to leave a review for this book on Amazon? I certainly appreciate your honest review.

Thank you very much and good luck!

Sincerely,

Wendy Oo

Printed in Great Britain
by Amazon